Killari 1993

The story of Rehabilitation village

---

*Story based on Real incident

Horror ! Yes this incident is beyond the Horror for the local citizens. Still Today the local citizens feel that experience of Horror earthquake. Killari is the small village in latur district of Maharashtra state in the country India.

The story I am going to share with you is Real.
When you Ask Maharashtra state citizens about killari village then they Replay you....
" Yes we know about the earthquake ".
Each citizens of Maharashtra knows about killari. The reason is that the

Horror earthquake was the first time in maharashtra state.
The story begins in 1993.
The year 1993 was the unknown Horror year for the local citizens of Killari village.
The Date was 30 September, The year was 1993 and The festival was " God

Ganesh visarjan." Note that the festival of "God Ganesh visarjan" was on 29th September 1993. An Earthquake boomed on Dawn of 30 September 1993. Before The date of 30 September local citizens of killari were busy in the preparation of "God

Ganesh Visarjan".
They also celebrated
this festival till late
night of 29
September 1993.
But they didn't know
The huge earthquake
coming towards the
Dawn of thirty
September of 1993.
All the people were
in deep sleep. They
didn't get a sense of
Earthquake.

But unfortunately nearby at 4 AM the earthquake boomed with a big sound and vibration. All the houses collapsed. Some of the people who got up in the early morning were saved from this calamity. But those who are in deep sleep are not

Remains in Good condition. Some of them died and some of them were still alive. The conditions of that time were very difficult and Horrible.

In this horrible condition the Rains began and it made it very difficult to save the people who were under the walls of their houses.

Many families were affected by this 1993 Earthquake.

Government tried to save the people and they were also successful in saving some of them. But those people who are under the deep soil, they don't remain alive.

Many families missed their dear ones due to the earthquake. It was a very sad full condition. But the people of Killari were faced courageously by this condition. After this calamity people are replaced at the other location. Name of that location was Killari pati. Today this location is the biggest marketplace for Killari marketers. All peoples of killari and nearby villages came to killari pati for shopping and purchasing goods. The centre of this earthquake under the earth crust is about 12 KM. Hence killari was the centre of Earthquake. Still some of the Resources of 1993 remain. Like collapsed Homes and other things. When you visit Killari village you feel the earthquake scene. But Today since 2020 Killari is an old village working on

development of
Lands.

One of the popular
temples known as "
Nilkantheshwar
Temple killari" was
the very Historical
temple.

This temple was very
big. The speciality of
this temple is its
very fresh Ground
and lots of greenery
trees.

And the very silent and natural environment of the temple.
God Shree Nilkantheshwar was very beautiful. Nilkantheshwar Temple also known as " Jagrut Devasthan" means very sensitive God. Nilkantheshwar listens to the

problems of their prayers and gives them instant solutions.

Because of the God Nilkantheshwar Killari is peaceful still today.

Every year in "Shravan '' Month that is in the Rainy season the fair of Nilkantheshwar temple was organised. Many peoples arounds the villages come to visit the temple of Nilkantheshwar. They receive a sense of Healthy hygiene. Nilkantheshwar temple trusts decorate the temple with dazzling lights and sound system.

Killari citizens visit the temple everyday. They believe they get a peaceful environment in the temple.
In the fair of Nilkantheshwar temple lots of playing instruments and shops have come. Many people take the chance to enjoy this fair by

playing different Games and shopping glowing products. Nilkantheshwar temple was developing regularly on the basis of the needs of the people. Nilkantheshwar temple trusts build two " Mangal Karyalaya" or wedding buildings

for marriage functions.
Every year hundreds of weddings take place in this temple Area.
Nilkantheshwar temple had plenty of water. But the new killari is still facing the problems of water. Some of the water suppliers provide water on the

money. Water suppliers Get the water from Nilkantheshawara Mandir and then they distribute it in Killari village. Nilkantheshawara Mandir provides food for people during the fair. They provide three meals to all the people who come to that temple.

Killari 1993 : the Story of rehabilitation village

They prepare Good Quality of meal for the people. Because of the helpful nature of Nilkantheshawara Mandir and Awesome environment hence it is popular in latur district.
Until we discussed the earthquake of 1993 and

Nilkantheshwar temple.
Now we are going to discuss the development of killari. How this village developed itself in the Marketing field. Killari on the way to a well -developed village in the category of marketing.

Most of the small
business making
More than 40,000 a
month.
Mostly in Killari
these are the
business available,
clothing shops,
shopping complex,
hotels , sweet marts,
 footwear,
stationary, groceries
shops, chicken
shops, drink shops,

Killari 1993 : the Story of rehabilitation village

photography, medicals, hospitals , fruit market, vegetable market and pan shops. Most profitable businesses are pan shops. Killari is a village where people love to chew nuts (supari).

Hence mostly pan shops are making Lots of profit.

Killari 1993 : the Story of rehabilitation village

Most trending businesses in Killari Are shopping malls and big grocery stores and also medical stores. Compared to 1993 in 2020 killari is boosting itself. There are some popular shops in Killari, like "Renuka". This is shopping mall

Which is mostly popular for clothes. Renuka is a modern clothing shop in the Killari region. They are making large amounts of profit because of their hard work.

Another one example of a modern grocery store is " Terana supermarket". This is the grocery shopping store. Killari continuously changes itself. Killari never stopped to improve its Brand identity. Many neighborhood village citizens come to Killari for shopping groceries and clothes.

Killari has also modern hospitals like "Sagar Hospital". This hospital is popular in Killari and out of the kilari. The Reason is the clean environment of hospitals and Good doctors and multi special services.

Sagar Hospital makes continuous changes to serve their patients. Here are some examples...." Sagar Hospital provides special files to their patients for keeping their hygiene record. This is how the killari Market makes lots of changes in the killari citizens' life.

Killari 1993 : the Story of rehabilitation village

Now we are going to discuss local government. The local politics is very competitive and Not so active.
Killari village going back because of killari village politics. Sarpanch of killari aren't Active. They don't work actively for their villagers.

Killari 1993 : the Story of rehabilitation village

Because of inappropriate politics Killari is still facing the Problem of Water. This is the major problem of this village.

Nowadays some of the Rich people of Killari are making their own source of water.

Only poor people's facing the problems

of water because they didn't have such an economy to make their own source of water. All the poor citizens depend on Tap water. But the water doesn't flow through the Tap pipe. It takes one and half months to get the water through the Tap.

It means local
political parties
don't solve problems
in Killari village.
They are just
Running behind
earning money and
doing some of the
work and showing
How they are good.
But they are not able
to solve the issues of
villagers. It's the

truth of Killari village.
But in the other field instead of local politics Killari Region made lots of improvements. Like the educational field. The field of education in the killari on the increasing rates. Many school institutions are

making lots of changes in their schools. They are allowing free education to the students. Like " Shivaji vidyalaya killari or junior college killari" and " Maharashtra vidyalaya killari or junior college". These institutions provide better education to their students. But the fact is they are just focusing on the Ranking system. They aren't able to take practical education to their students.

Still there are so many issues in the school system. In the category of teaching. Like some of the teachers who are teaching a specific subject they are not able to understand the demand of students. Students want practical education. They want practice based education. They need different competitions. They like to attend different Science

exhibitions and many more.
Students of killari are demanding a skill Based education system. But these institutions don't provide High Quality of education.
According to Today's Q Magazine Report. The students of killari are the most copied students in

Maharashtra state. The reason behind this is....

" Rankings system of schools and their publicity". The Regional schools of Killari are showing themselves How they are providing Better education compared to others. But the fact is " teachers of these schools provide copies to their students during board Exams". Now you are thinking why Maharashtra Board doesn't know this. The fact is " the Maharashtra board Zp teachers who came to inspect the exams are also

joined with these schools."
Many students are against the copy but the Teachers make it compulsory to do copy during board exams. It's really an inappropriate education. But it's a hidden fact of killari educational institutions.

I am Requesting these institutions please stop this. What are you going to do ? And what are you achieving ? You are growing only garbage in the brain of students. You are making them illegal. You are breaking the rules of the Maharashtra state board of education.

What you think the Ranking of your school makes you popular. It's your fault Ranking doesn't make your school popular. Honest work and passionate teaching to make their students bright futures.. hence be Honest towards the education system.

Now we are
discussing the
atmosphere of the
killari.
Killari has a better
atmosphere.
Atmospheric
changes depends on
The season changes.
Killari has a very
perfect environment
to live a better life.
Now we are going to
discuss about

Future of killari. According to statistics, killari is growing continuously. The Killari market has the potential to boost the economy of Killari village. The future of killari is bright. Many killari citizens predict that killari is the district level village. According to the citizens of Killari it is the biggest village and has productivity like tulaka level. Hence they are demanding the government " killari should be declared as Taluka ''. Considering the Growth of market and education institutions Killari has a bright future. We are wishing Killari should be the biggest city in the future.

End

About book

This is a short book written by The youngest Author Bk Murumbe. Author Bk Murumbe is a citizen of killari. This book is written on the

Killari 1993 : the Story of rehabilitation village

observation of a 10 years period. Bk Murumbe observed this village from their childhood.

Bk Murumbe decided to put the history and future of his village in front of Global citizens.

<u>About Author</u>

Hello my self Bk Murumbe. I am a citizen of killari. I observed the killari marketplace and politics of killari and also the educational institution of killari village. I just listened

to the earthquake of 1993.

On the basis of my observation data I wrote this book and published it in the world. I wish every global citizen should listen to my village Story through my book. My purpose is they will visit my village and give their

Reviews about my village. _______|

<u>Terms and conditions</u>

The book written under the general observation. Hence content written in this book are the observation Based opinions.

Their is no hates speech included in this book. This book owned by Author BK Murumbe. Every page of this book is owned by author and has 100% rights to distribute it. Don't copy the contents of the book because it is under the author Bk Murumbe.

*If any misleading content in this book then Readers are able to inform the author through the *contact page.*

Contact

Please inform us If there are any errors in our book content. We like to hear from you and we are trying to make our book error free.

Email us : todaysq100@gmail.com

Follow the author on Amazon author page :
https://amazon.com/author/bkmurambe
Thanks for reading this book. Share it with your friends and family. Thank you.

Killari 1993 photos

Killari 1993 : the Story of rehabilitation village

Killari 1993 : the Story of rehabilitation village

Important Highlights of 1993 earthquake

Total damage	$280M-1.3B	magnitude	6.2 M_w
Dead	9,748	Depth	10 KM
Injured	30,000	**MAX intensity**	Severe

Killari 1993 : the Story of rehabilitation village

www.ingramcontent.com/pod-product-compliance
Lightning Source LLC
Chambersburg PA
CBHW070048260726
48658CB00002B/786